DUBLIN
TECHNOLOGICAL
UNIVERSITY DUBLIN

Donated to

**Visual Art Degree
Sherkin Island**

D1438990

THE LONG GOODBYE

Limited Edition No: 000975

THE LONG GOODBYE

A cartoon tribute to a Taoiseach

MARTYN TURNER

IRISH TIMES BOOKS
DUBLIN

First published February 1992
by Irish Times Books,
11-15 D'Olier Street, Dublin

ISBN 0 907011 19 5

Distribution: Irish Times General Services. Telephone (01) 679 2022 Ext 309.
Printed in Republic of Ireland by Genprint, Dublin.

INTRODUCTION

"I suppose", said the whole world in unison, "that you cartoonists must be having a Field Day at the moment?" Truth to tell, we cartoonists never have Field Days. We did try to have a picnic once, but the plans fell through. Life with Charlie, for cartoonists, was no picnic either, despite appearances to the contrary.

Rule number one for political cartoonists is that you are interested in the politics of a situation, not the personalities. But for the last 20 years, since the Arms Trial, the politics of CJH and his personality tended to be one and the same thing. By all accounts he was an imaginative, progressive and competent minister in the sixties but for the last 13 years he was just another politician whose main preoccupation was to retain the occupation of Taoiseach.

Politics, which is what political cartoonists are mainly interested in, were almost entirely absent from CJH's public life in the last ten years. He sat on the fence during the divorce referendum, he botched the contraception issue, he opposed the Anglo-Irish Agreement in opposition and then embraced it in government. According to Mary O'Rourke he got round to doing something about the economy in 1987, although he had dramatically outlined the problem in a speech in 1979. No grand designs were implemented, no major reforms, just government on idle and a string of scandalous allegations and internal Fianna Fáil rows. So many Fianna Fáil rows that during the compilation of this book we were hard pressed to identify which was which.

And so political issues went out of the window and were replaced with Charlieism. The survival of Mr Haughey became a political issue in itself. The cartoonists response was to create a political symbol for this political issue. In my case the symbol was a tiny man with a vast red nose, hair that ascended to heaven and thick dark eyebrows.

It is part of the magic of caricature that someone can be identified by features that he doesn't possess. Edward Heath was drawn with a Concorde nose by all and sundry. He doesn't have a Concorde nose, some cartoonist invented it and everyone else copied it. I was once congratulated on a caricature I had done of Charlie. I couldn't remember the drawing I was being praised for so I looked it up. Charlie doesn't appear in the drawing. There were just two hairs sticking out of the bottom right-hand corner. The rest had been filled in by someone's mind.

A beautician from across the water was once interviewed on the Late Late Show. She was shown photographs of well known Irish personalities and asked to improve their looks. She drew a pair of my Mr Haughey's black eyebrows on the Taoiseach's photograph. For years I had been unwittingly enhancing his appearance.

But having the politician, and his character, as the political issue itself isn't very rewarding. Commentating on personalities doesn't get us anywhere, and clearly didn't get Mr Haughey anywhere either, although it took a long time for us all to discover it.

Richard Nixon was pretty good on foreign policy, at times. But all anyone remembers about Richard Nixon is Watergate and his seven o'clock shadow. Charles Haughey, to judge from his political obituaries, was imaginative, intelligent, gifted, humorous and able. Yet he'll be remembered as the enigma of the Arms trial, the Doherty tapes, the phone call to the Arus. He'll be remembered as the man who made Noel Davern Minister for Education.

We drawers of politics are in for harder times now our Richard Nixon has gone. It's back to politics. But we can take comfort in the thought that if the Richard Nixon of Irish politics has gone then, maybe, the Ronald Reagan of Irish politics is just around the corner.

Martyn Turner, February 1992

own favourite . . . on visiting Belfast.

1979: Jack Lynch resigns.

1979: Fresh from a free toothbrush scheme, Mr Haughey faces a hostile Dáil.

1980

1981: *The first heave, from Kildare.*

1981

1982: Bugging

followed by more trouble in the ranks.

1982: Paranoia.

another failed heave.

INNUENDO
INTRIGUE
INSULTS
INQUIRIES
INVESTIGATIONS

IN

OUT

OUT OF OFFICE

1984

Problems with the special relationship.

1983: THE RESUMPTION OF THE SPECIAL RELATIONSHIP AFTER FIANNA FAIL ELECTION VICTORY

The Mariner.

1984: Another revolt.

O Malley leaves.

1987: An election poster.

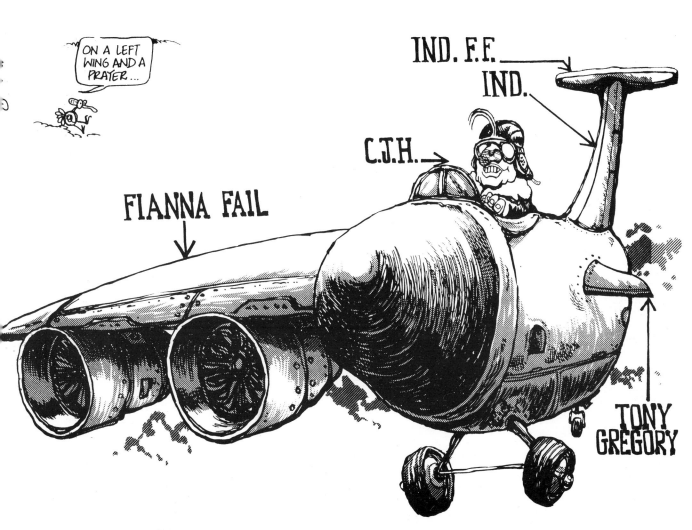

Our new stable Government – an early design concept.

THE PLANE PEOPLE of IRELAND

1988: Mr Haughey goes to Australia, and comes back.

THE CAT'S BACK

1988: Mr Haughey goes into hospital, and leaves.

An affinity with birds: Jury's get a hawk

Kerry got an eagle.

1989: The election result.

1989: The negotiations.

The Marching Season

REMEMBER
12TH JULY 1989
The Battle of the Dail

Side

Front

1990: The Presidential Election aftermath.

LEADER-SHIP

P.E.S.

GREENCORE

BUDGET OVER-RUN

CONDOM BILL

P.D. NEGOTIATIONS

Autumn 1991.

.....CONTROVERSIAL SEWERAGE PIPELINE BYPASSING THE TAOISEACH

GREENCORE MEETINGS

JUST ANOTHER
LITTLE BLOW

SOMEONE'S HELICOPTERS COMING HOME TO ROOST

Woody Allen tells a story about his father, who had the skittle concession on the Boardwalk in Atlantic City. Following a terrible storm most of Atlantic City and all of the Boardwalk was destroyed, levelled to the ground. Mr. Allen's skittles were the only things left standing. I don't seem to be able to get that story out of my head, at the moment, for some reason. ■Martyn Turner■

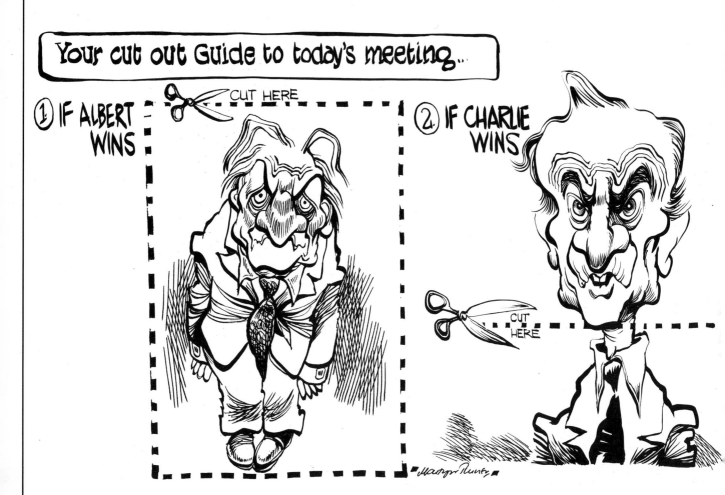

MIN. for ENVIRONMENT

AN TAOISEACH

MINISTER FOR FINANCE

MIN. for GAELTACHT

MINISTER FOR GOING WITH DIGNITY

...AND THEN, FOR A FEW GLORIOUS MOMENTS THE CABINET WAS UNITED LIKE IT HAD NEVER BEEN BEFORE........

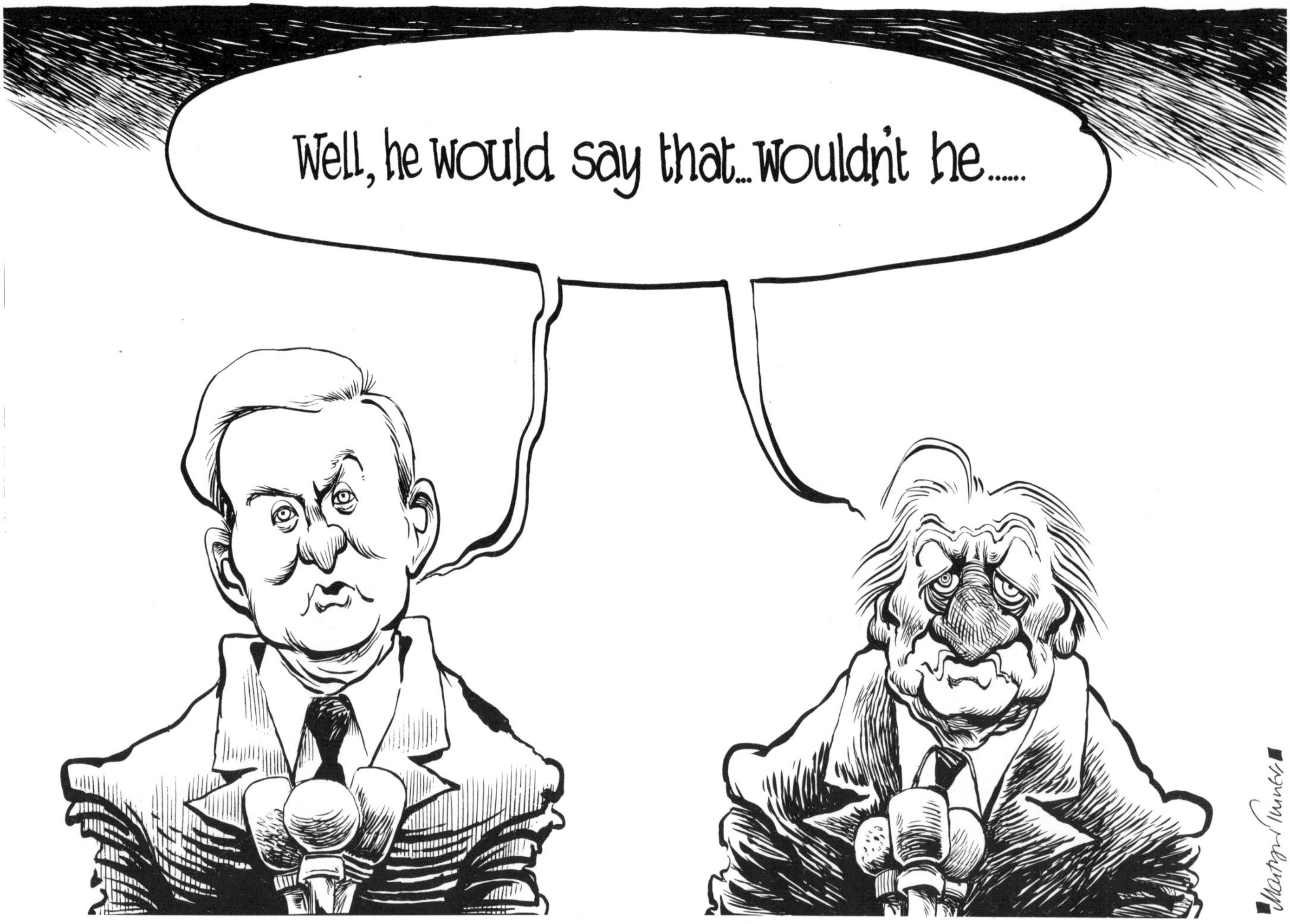
Well, he would say that...wouldn't he......

DIGNITY

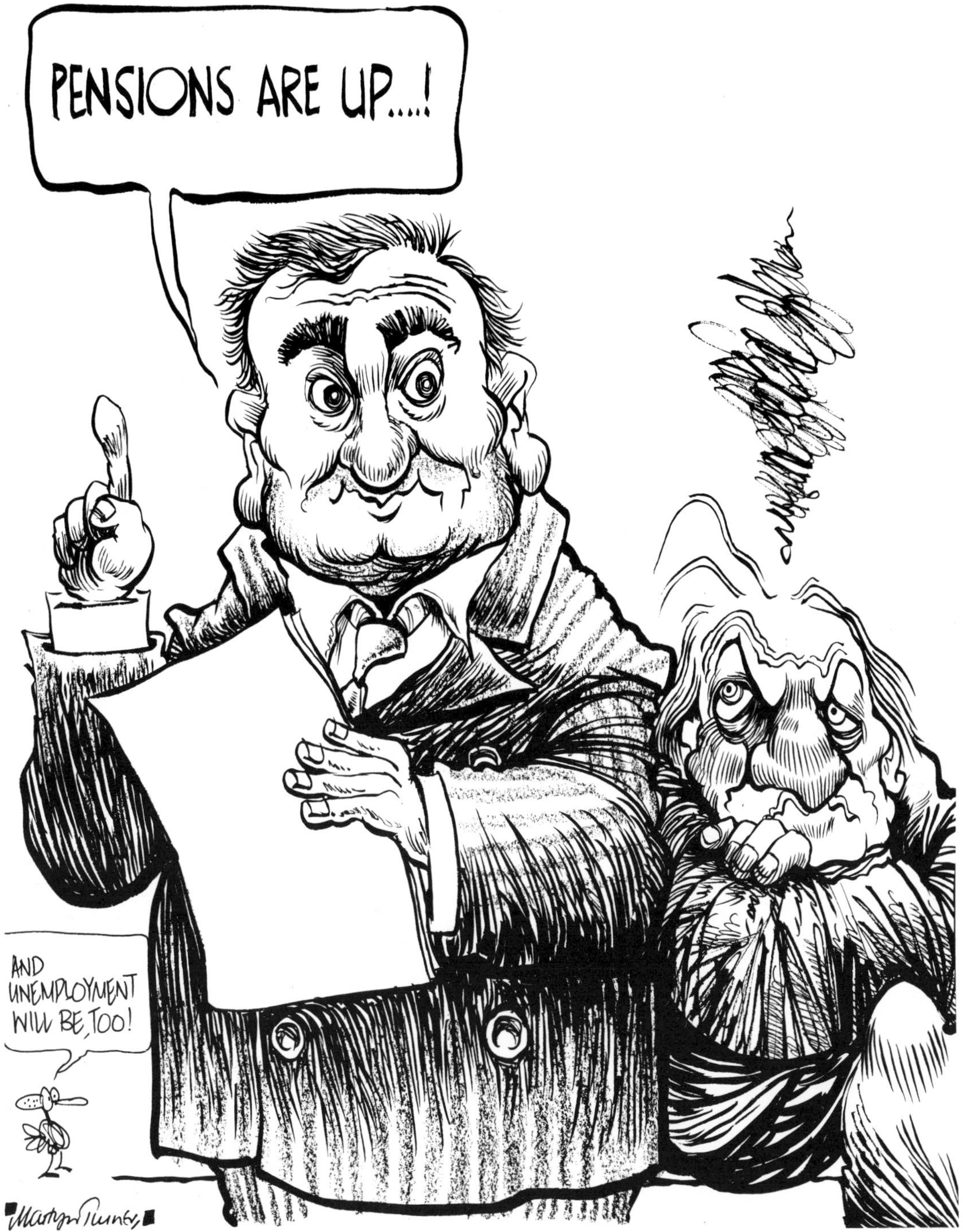
PENSIONS ARE UP....!
AND UNEMPLOYMENT WILL BE, TOO!
Martyn Turner